Copyright © 2013
by Delila Mayer

All rights reserved. No part of the material protected by this copyright notice may be reproduced or
utilized in any form or by any means, electronic or mechanical, including photocopying, recording or by any informational storage and retrieval system
without written permission from the copyright owner.

ISBN-13: 978-1492301608
ISBN-10: 1492301604

First Edition, 2013

Published by
Groundwaters Publishing, LLC

P.O. Box 50, Lorane, Oregon 97451
http://www.groundwaterspublishing.com

*"When you win, you praise the Lord.
When you lose, you praise the Lord."*

~Ryan

Ryan Mayer

May 26, 1969 - April 1, 2010

*My Son Died and He is Still with Me by
the Power of the Holy Spirit*

By his Mother, Delila Mayer

My Son Died and He is Still with Me by the Power of the Holy Spirit

~ This is what Love looks like~

Dedicated to our Blessed Mother Mary, who came to get Ryan at the moment of his death and carried him to Jesus to be with Him forever.

From my mother's heart, I would like to share with you the life and passing of our dear son, Ryan Mayer, who died April 1, 2010, after battling brain cancer for three years. Ryan was born May 26, 1969, and died at age 40, leaving a young wife, three children under seven years of age, his Mom and Dad and four siblings with their families. His great love for us and for our Lord, as well as his courage, made our sad path – our Via Dolorosa – our way of the cross – bearable. Our hearts were totally broken. I still cannot say, "Thanks be to God," for this particular, excruciating painful trial, but I can say, "He, my Lord and Savior, Jesus Christ, has been faithful and loving to me every step of the way and I live because He lives within me. Jesus Christ is so good to us and His way throughout all of this continues to be revealed."

Ryan's Childhood

Ryan died as he lived, trusting in Jesus Christ, his Lord and Savior. He was only 40 years old when he went home to be with his Lord. Ryan was our third child out of five; he was a middle child. He played that role well. We had four children in 4 years and 11 months, so it was natural that he found his grandfather, who lived very close to us, to be his mentor and the one who really believed in him. Many times we didn't know where Ryan was. His shoes were still in the doorway, but he was gone. We knew he was probably with Grandpa Mayer and in good hands. Grandpa Mayer taught him what was important in life and what was acceptable to God and what wasn't. He was a hardworking man and a faithful Catholic. He worked hard and he taught Ryan to work hard and to respect women. Ryan knew that having premarital sex was not acceptable as a man of God. His Grandfather, without even talking with him about it, instilled it in him. Grandpa Mayer always said about Ryan, whom he called "Rynie," that he was never scared of anything. Both loved the farm, the land and the horses.

Grandpa taught him to ride and they would go on camping trips to Medora with the horses and sleep in the pickup near the horses. I remember sending notes along for every day of the week when he was there, just so he would have a touch of my heart while he was gone. Grandma always made cookies for them, too, as a treat from the farm and from her heart. Ryan always knew he was especially precious to his grandfather, Frank F. Mayer. I personally was grateful for that because I was always busy with the three other children.

Ryan grew up with a cousin who lived very close to us. His name was Shane Mayer and he was only three months older than Ryan. When Ryan was born, Grandma Bertha Mayer prophesied that now Shane will have a best friend. And so that's the way it was. They were always playing together and really enjoyed each other and looked forward to going to school together and being teenagers together. They didn't get into much trouble except for one time they started a bale of hay on fire and it was pretty scary for both of them.

Ryan was an above-average student and really didn't want to be the top of the class. He would always say, "That's good enough." He was very level-headed about life. He took the hard times with the good, always looking for the balance. I'm wondering if, because the first two siblings before him did so very well academically, that he just didn't want to be an academic star also. He just really wanted to be his own person and have his own life.

His teen years were not a concern for me because he had Shane, his cousin and best friend. They always spent lots of time together, snowmobiling and having fun on the farm with Grandpa and our animals. In my heart's way of thinking, I always felt the Lord took special care of Ryan with a protection-umbrella over him, sheltering him from the hard knocks of life.

Ryan always enjoyed farming with his father, especially – working the fields and, when we had cattle, working the cattle at roundup time. In high school, his only aim was to beat his father's crop-judging score in FFA. He succeeded.

He was about six feet tall. He played basketball for two years in high school and all of us in the town remember him playing a scrimmage game when there was two seconds left in the game and he threw a shot from the middle of the court and made it and won the game. He was more shocked than we were that he did it. He loved football, but didn't play it long in high school because he basically wasn't aggressive enough and he was needed on the farm.

The professional football team that he really loved was the Green Bay Packers. Locally, he especially delighted in watching his Mott Wild Fire Team win a state championship in 2007. I remember, in regard to that game, the Lord getting me up at 2:00 a.m., four days before the state championship game, and asking me to write to each of the team members. I told the Lord it was 2:00 a.m. and that if He did not tell me what to write, I would go back to bed. I remember I had lots of pass-it-on cards that said, *The Lord Thy God is with Thee*, and so I waited for the Lord to give me what I should write on them to the 35 football players. And, so, this is what He gave me: "Dear ....., I want you to *know that I am praying for you; that if you will play this game for the Lord with no cheap shots and ask Jesus to come into your heart, to take over your life and to run your life, that He will do that. All you have to do is just ask Him to show you your sins and be 100% sorry for them. You watch! You wait! You'll see! The Wild Fire of God will come alive in you."*

I remember praying in the spirit, in tongues, that whole game. (see *Appendix*) I think my blood pressure was 300 on both ends. As the Napoleon team, from Napoleon, North Dakota, came onto the field, I knew this would be a David and Goliath fight. The Napoleon boys were Norwegian and German and were all big wrestlers. Our Mott boys are little Germans, but quick. We had just lost our two best players from injuries. We needed a miracle, just like David did. Believe it or not, the Lord did that for us and by two fumbles, we won the State Championship. One of the fumbles was even into the end zone and one of the kids just happened to catch it. At the victory gathering afterwards Charlie Crane said, "Thanks, Delila, for praying for us." All I could say was "Amen" and cried.

Ryan Finds a Wife

In our family we had wonderful, inspired weddings. My husband and I always prayed the kids would marry people who loved the Lord and were Catholic. The Lord heard those prayers and each marriage was a great gift to us.

When Ryan was ready to be married, he had waited a long time for not only a good wife, but he wanted "*a magnificent one*," and *those* are his words. Lori was given to him when he was about 30 years old and he was very blessed, but as he would have said, "She is Lutheran," so that proposed a challenge to him to really understand his Catholic faith. When he would come to wheat harvest with us, he would bring along teaching CDs of Dr. Scott

Hahn, a former Presbyterian minister who has become a Catholic author, theologian and apologist. Ryan devoured everything of Dr. Hahn's work and, of course, shared it with Lori. He sent Lori to a Father DeGrandis seminar at Mandan, North Dakota, Spirit of Life Church, and she was with us for a weekend then. It was there that she learned the importance of the Mass and grew to want more of the Catholic faith.

At one point, they did break up over the Catholic issue, as she was a very good Lutheran. I remember her calling me and being so sad and I remembered what Kimberly Hahn's father had said to her as she struggled with becoming a Catholic after Dr. Scott Hahn's conversion to the Catholic faith:"*Kimberly, just pray three things: 1) I'll go where you want me to go, Lord. 2) I'll be what you want me to be, and, 3) I'll do what you want me to do.*" I told her she really wouldn't want to honestly pray that at first, but to ask the Lord to change her heart. It was after she prayed that prayer that she was willing to go to the Franciscan University in Steubenville, Ohio, to a young people's conference on defending the faith. After that weekend, she told Ryan she wanted to become a good Catholic and please the Lord.

I remember I was at Clearwater, Florida, at the time, earning a certificate in Spiritual Direction in the school of the *Spiritual Exercises* of St. Ignatius Loyola. One of my teachers told me to ask the Blessed Mother, Mary, to intercede for her conversions and to pray a rosary every day for that intention. I did. The Blessed Mother brought Lori into the church which she cherishes today. Ryan would have not married her if she would not have become Catholic and it had to be from her heart. He said he wanted his children to be raised with the seven Sacraments and the word of God. It was interesting to note that for the love of the Church and Jesus alive in the Sacraments, that he would only marry a Catholic woman and that he would eventually die on Holy Thursday which is the day of the institution of the Holy Priesthood and the Holy Eucharist.

Ryan and Lori Marry

Their wedding was such a precious gift to our family! They asked everyone in the wedding party to go to confession on the night of the wedding rehearsal. I remember going to confession with Fr. Anderl and just being so grateful that we would have a holy wedding, pleasing unto the Lord. The day we gave Ryan away was one of the happiest in my life. Ryan's father, Francis, was his best man and Lori's mother, Judy, was her matron of honor. Ryan had two brothers and really couldn't choose between them to be his best man, so he asked his father whom he admired very much. To see this couple really love God's word and the Eucharist with all their hearts was a great joy to the whole family. Lori's parents were most gracious in loving Ryan and accepting him into their family. I remember a picture taken that day with all of us in the wedding party rejoicing with our hands uplifted in joy for what the Lord had done that day in the Sacrament of Holy Matrimony. A former Lutheran Pastor from Lori's hometown softly said to us, "Please take care of our little girl," and I said, "Lori will be a wonderful Catholic because she was such a good Lutheran." And we embraced each other. He felt as if he was losing her and I felt his pain.

I remember at the wedding supper, my husband, Francis, who was the best man, told Ryan, "This is the day you'll love Lori the least. You'll learn to love her sacrificially and give everything."

Ryan and Lori were a great joy to our hearts as they built a new home in Casselton, North Dakota, a 4½ hour drive from our home in Mott, North Dakota. Ryan worked for CoBank and was a credit analyst for that firm. They designed their own home and were open to having a baby soon after their marriage. They were married September 21, 2002, and Matthew Francis came the day they moved into their new home, February 28, 2004. He came six weeks early and was in the newborn intensive care unit for awhile, but was a beautiful baby boy who Ryan delighted in as his first son.

They grew in the word of God in the Catholic faith together as they attended Mass weekly and came before the Blessed Sacrament often in Adoration. They continued to ask the Lord to show them a mission for their marriage they could share. By the time they married, the Lord opened up a Premarital Counseling ministry for them, helping couples of mixed faiths be united in the Catholic faith. In fact, a week before Ryan died, he and Lori met with a couple who both wanted to be Catholic, but who had a lot of questions.

Brain Cancer, May 2007

A second son was born to Ryan and Lori on July 18, 2007, while Ryan had cancer. I so admired Lori, who was pregnant at the time, for her trusting the Lord with his outcome and living *Proverbs* 3.5, "*Trust in the Lord with all your heart and lean not on your own understanding . In all thy ways acknowledge Him and He will bring it to pass.*" Lori lived on this. It was an extremely hard time for her and for all of us when we learned Ryan had cancer of the brain. We lived that scripture to the fullest. Ryan had surgery and they removed a tumor from the left side of his brain. They said it was the size of a peanut before the surgery on May 15, 2007, but it came out to be even larger. It gave me great comfort that the surgery was on St. Isidore's feast day, the patron saint of farmers. The cancer's name was oligoastrocytoma and it was in Stage 3 which means it had not spread into the rest of Ryan's body. Stage 4 is end stage cancer.

Ryan lived in hope that it was nothing when he started to have short, intense headaches that were not getting better after seeing a chiropractor. His regular physician also gave him a clean bill of health. He was only 37 years old. He was such an optimistic soul and really hoped his frequent headaches would cease, but when, one day at work, he tried to speak to his secretary but could not get any words out, he knew he was in trouble. He was finally able to speak and he told his secretary this and she said she would drive him to the hospital. Ryan was feeling better by then and said he would drive himself. He drove himself to the Emergency Room where they did a CT scan and said there was definitely swelling in his brain and they couldn't believe he was standing there on his own.

They wanted to send him by ambulance downtown to the hospital to do an MRI, but he told them he would drive himself just as he did to get to the ER. He stayed the night and all we knew was they would monitor his swelling. Lori came the next day, anticipating taking him home, only to find out he was having brain surgery that afternoon! He didn't see any urgency in calling his parents, but she called us and although shocked, we were on our way to Fargo immediately to be with them.

The day of the surgery was hard, but we had learned to trust the Lord in all things, even our son who really didn't belong to us, but to God and His purposes. As we gave Ryan back to the Lord, as we did with our children every day, we just praised Jesus for taking care of him and trusted all would work out for God's purposes. We praised the Lord in the Spirit and He did give us peace that passed all understanding which is a miracle for those who can believe in divine intervention. He picked us up and took us through the pain as we praised Him and committed the problem totally to Him. That's our God! This is what love looks like.

After the surgery, Ryan needed chemotherapy and radiation as they aggressively fought the cancer. The treatments made him sick. And, as I heard him struggle with all of this, all I could say was, "Lord, you know how to take him through this." I continuously "offered it up," as we Catholics do, uniting all our sufferings with the sufferings of Christ on the Cross for the good of all and for the salvation of all. That was the hope I had as his mother as I also prayed for his total healing.

Remission

The Lord answered that prayer in mysterious ways. He was well for two years after the surgery and treatments. Lori and Ryan both wanted a daughter and asked the Lord for that gift. Maria Jeane was born February 6, 2009, after the Lord helped Lori understand the Blessed Mother would intercede for this little girl to Jesus. Being a new Catholic, Lori was starting to understand the Communion of Saints, the Great Cloud of Witnesses, who loved to intercede with Jesus for our needs. Lori promised the Blessed Mother that her little girl would be named in honor of her if she were a girl. She kept that promise as they gave her the name Maria and gave her the middle name, Jeane, which was her mother's middle name. She was a beautiful, little redhead, someone I always wanted to have as a granddaughter. Only Ryan and Lori could have given me a redhead and it was the last physical thing he could do for me before he went to Heaven. Now I am so thankful for his gifts of praying and interceding for us because loves goes on forever and can be this way. He is there in the Lord's presence caring and helping us.

Recurrence

Ryan's recurrence of brain cancer was in the fall of 2009, when he was once again at work. This time, he could not remember where the water fountain was. He was alone in the office, so he just waited it out and came home as normal to tell Lori. He hoped it was nothing, but Lori urged him to tell his cancer doctor and schedule an MRI. The cancer had come back with a vengeance, so he went to Mayo Clinic in Rochester, Minnesota, where they did surgery, but they did not get it all. It had traveled from the left side of the brain to the middle and to the right. The doctors wanted to do chemotherapy and radiation again, but Ryan did not want to do this because his chances of recovery were very slim. The doctors said this was precious time before, most likely, death. He drove home from Mayo Clinic, just a few days after his second surgery and bravely embraced life and confronted death. He had heard about Dr. Buzyenski's Clinic in Houston, Texas, and wanted to try the "recreation of cells" therapy there. Lori and Maria, who was still nursing, accompanied him to Houston to see if this procedure would work. It was an extremely hard time for both of them as there was little hope for recovery. Lori wanted to go home for Christmas, so I went to Texas to be with Ryan for 11 days.

It was our last Christmas together and it was most precious to my heart as we talked out many things and went to Holy Mass often before he started his treatments. The treatments were difficult. As I am not a registered nurse, I had to learn the best I could to help him. I could see he was getting weaker and that Lori had to learn the method so Ryan had to call her to come down again after Christmas. It was hard for me to leave him and for Lori to come because she had to quit nursing her year-old baby.

So, my trip back to North Dakota was disturbing, to say the least. I wanted to be with my husband and family to celebrate a late Christmas with them at a resort in Detroit Lakes, Minnesota, but I wanted to be with Ryan also. Another trial was before me to learn to trust with all my heart and to not lean on my own understanding.

The night we all got together at the resort, I couldn't sleep, and so I prayed in tongues all night, the perfect prayer for those who pray in the spirit. About 3:00 a.m., I felt there was a presence in my bedroom. I have never had a vision before, so I really wondered what this was all about. All I knew was that it was a peaceful presence. I recognized it was St. Anthony, one of my favorite saints, who always helped me find things when I asked him to intercede for me and to go to Jesus for me. I saw his "tonsured hairline" and I knew it was him as he is pictured this way in the Catholic prayer books. Then I saw Padre Pio and he did speak to me and he said, "Mother, do not worry. Seek and you shall find. Ask and it shall be given unto you. Knock and it shall be opened unto you." I had been praying the Efficacious Novena (see *Appendix*) to the Sacred Heart of Jesus for some time and I realized St. Pio received this novena everyday for all those who asked for his prayers so he had been praying for me.

So, I asked with great faith, for not only peace that would pass all understanding, but for joy in this trial. I asked for it all. After I asked for it all, St. Theresa of Lisieux appeared with a bouquet of flowers with a cross in the flowers and she handed them to me. After that I knew Ryan's body would probably soon die and that he would carry the cross to the end and so would I, but the presence of God would be with us. The sweet smell of roses was given to me as a great consolation and a reminder of the Lord's love for me and my family in this most sad ordeal and for God's presence and purpose in it all. I had been praying the St. Therese of the Child Jesus' Novena Rose Prayer (see *Appendix*) for years and understood that she gives flowers from Heaven to those who believe she will intercede for their need. I was so surprised to receive a whole bouquet of fresh roses in the spirit from her when I had this vision with Saints Padre Pio and Anthony.

Also, Ryan had two favorite saints, Saint Francis of Assisi, per his middle name, and St. Theresa of Lisieux of the Child Jesus – of the roses from Heaven. Both saints were very humble people and knew the way to have an abundant life was to live simply and to walk in God's little way for them. He was learning how to follow them!

What I realize now is that all the prayers we had prayed over the years, had prepared our hearts for this sad trial, and had, line upon line, here a little and there a little, strengthened us in our spirit, in the Christ within us, so that we could stand in this storm with Jesus Christ our Lord and Savior. Through the years of prayers and of spiritual disciplines, we realized our gradual transformation into warriors and servants so Jesus could trust us with such great sadness and distress and have meaning come out of it in His way.

My dear husband Francis and I have prayed the Cardinal Mecier's prayer, "The Secret of Sanctity," for years that gave us an abode of peace and even joy and tranquility in this storm. The prayer is *"O Holy Spirit, soul of my soul, I adore You. Enlighten, guide, strengthen and console me. Tell me what I ought to do and command me to do it. I promise to be submissive in everything that You permit to happen to me, only show me what is Your will."* Cardinal Mercier promised, *"Your life will pass happily and serenely. Consolations will abound even in the midst of troubles. Grace will be given in proportion to the trial as well as strength to bear it, bringing you to the gates of Paradise full of merit."* He especially emphasized in it that *"This submission to the Holy Spirit is the Secret of Sanctity."*

It was about this time that we also realized that being faithful to the teachings of the Catholic Church including our weekly Mass attendance where we received the body, blood, soul and divinity of our Lord and Savior Jesus Christ, gave us so many graces that came alive for us as we totally trusted the Lord with our son and his life. Great peace was given to us. Who are we to trust but Him! There is nowhere else to go when all things fail.

The story of Joseph and the many-colored coat came to mind often. What Satan started for evil, God will work for good. We did not understand it all. We could not rely on our own understanding, but we could trust God who made Ryan for himself and who gave him to our family for his time here on Earth.

Ryan's Death

As Ryan grew worse, he came home from Texas and went through a very hard time of trusting the Lord for the miracle of saving his life. He wondered, "Why me?" when he had tried so very hard to follow the Lord. He was very angry at God and the medical people, but worked it through to trust again. He received the grace to accept that God knew best. He went to confession and received peace, the peace that passes all understanding. He was ready to die and to go home to get his reward. I remember the day he died. He called out for me and said, "Mom." I told him I was there and that the Blessed Mother was coming to get him soon to take him to Jesus forever. I saw him smile. That was the last time I saw him smile.

He was breathing heavily by now and had morphine to help him. A Priest friend of ours came to say the Rosary which Ryan loved so much and said almost daily. Ryan knew that as he said the Rosary, the Blessed Mother would always take his heart back to the heart of Jesus and mercy for him. When Ryan was young, when he said the Rosary, he always had intentions for each decade and would tell me about them. It was always touching to me, that he believed the Blessed Mother would always work it out with Jesus for the good of all those concerned.

The Divine Mercy Chaplet (see *Appendix*) was next led in song by the choir director from Ryan's church. This beautiful devotion promises that Jesus will stand between the dying person and the enemy fighting for his soul. This also was one of Ryan's favorite prayers and he always prayed it during Adoration.

The Litany of the Saints was sung (see *Appendix*) and as Ryan took his last breath, I saw St. Francis and St. Theresa come for him with open arms. I also saw a Cloud of Witnesses behind him whom I did not recognize, but I knew it was a cloud of Saints, radiant beings, coming to welcome him home.

I then saw a great light, a pure light; it was radiant. I thought it was Jesus coming for Ryan, but it wasn't. It was his Blessed Mother. She said, "Come, Son, let's go home to Jesus forever." This is an interesting part. Ryan loved snowmobiles. There was a snowmobile present and I don't know if Mary came on it, but I do know that Ryan would have loved to have gone to Heaven on a snowmobile and perhaps he did with the Blessed Mother. And, so, as Ryan took his last breath, the nurse came in to check his heart beat and surprisingly enough, it did not quit for 20 minutes. And, he died, Mott time, during the Divine Mercy hour and during the time he usually spent in Adoration.

We left Lori with Ryan so she could be with him alone and each of us cried and hugged each other in the hall. It was a very emotional time, but surprisingly enough, there was peace in it, His peace in it. I called my husband who had gone home to buy a cemetery plot for Ryan at St. Stephens Church where he had been baptized 40 years earlier. He would be buried so very near to his beloved Grandfather Frank and his Grandmother Bertha. Lori was extremely kind to give his body back to us to be buried on the prairie that he loved so much. It was this great kindness that caused me to really weep. Ryan was buried six weeks later, due to a terrible winter with totally frozen ground, on Pentecost eve, May 22, 2010.

Some Special Thoughts

It was very meaningful that Ryan be buried on this day because when he was six years old, he asked Jesus to baptize him with the Holy Spirit and in Fire for his own Pentecost. (*Luke* 3.16) He asked for all the gifts, including the gift of tongues (I *Corinthians* 12), but the one gift I noticed he had profoundly been given was the gift of knowledge.

Daily, his father would call the family together at 7:30 p.m., take the phone receiver off the hook and call for family prayer time. We had just received the Baptism in the Holy Spirit in May of 1972, and it changed our hearts completely to see how precious we were to the Lord and how He loved us completely. So, my husband, as the spiritual head of the family, deigned we would have a family prayer time. The two of us always had a Catholic Bible study every morning and so he wanted to share what we had learned with our family. I'm the teacher in the family, but I realized, after many mistakes of trying to teach, that when Francis taught, the kids would really listen to him. We had daily prayers and then Francis would teach by God's word and then we would wait in silence for the Lord to talk with us in our spirits. It was at that time we realized Ryan's special gift of knowledge because he would say and know things impossible for him to know. I remember asking him how he got the message about why we should buy a piece of land and he, as a matter-of-fact, said, "The Lord just told me." He was so sure of that still small voice.

As I look back over his life, I can see that he really tried to listen to the Lord and walk in newness of grace each day. The Baptism of the Holy Spirit gave him the grace to do the hard things as a teenager. He decided never to drink or dishonor women. He and his cousin, Shane, hung together and enjoyed holy things, things that gave life to them. Ryan attended North Dakota State University in Fargo, North Dakota, and received a degree in agricultural economics. He really didn't want to go to college. He wanted to stay home and farm with his father, but we told him he needed to widen his horizons and develop his talents in college. He was a part of a SEARCH group, a teen peer Christian ministry, and he made 35 weekend retreats with them and was a spiritual director for one of them. As I look back over his life, I am so grateful he had that SEARCH group to grow and mature with. They helped him to serve the Body of Christ in the Farm House Fraternity he chose to be a part of. It was a dry house with only men who respected women. Later on in his life, he was on a financial board for Farm House as an adult.

Ryan became a Knight of Columbus and was the Grand Knight of the Fargo council for a year. His Uncle Lee was a Grand Knight before him and was a good example for him. Ryan learned to pray about everything, committing everything to the Lord and thanking him for everything before it came.

His funeral memory cards said, "*When you win, you praise the Lord. When you lose, you praise the Lord.*" He understood the Lord knows best. He was tested in that statement to the end. James 1.12 is a scripture emphasized in his Bible and that scripture is "*Happy the man who holds out to the end through trial. Once he has been proved, he will receive the crown of life the Lord has promised to those who love him."* (*New American Bible*, the Bible Ryan had). Ryan deeply realized he had received Jesus as his Savior by faith as a little boy, but needed to live out the life of grace and mercy and forgiveness to the end. He had to run his race, faithful to the end, on the course Jesus had laid out for him. He realized he had to be "pure in spirit" to see his Lord and that he should be living the beatitudes. *Matthew* 5.8 says "*Blessed are the pure in heart for they shall see God.*" He often prayed, "*Lord, create a clean heart in me and renew a right spirit within me,*" like King David prayed.

Ryan's Funeral

Ryan's funeral was on April 5, 2010, on Easter Monday, in the newly dedicated St. Anne and St. Joachim church which was decorated with Easter Joy, a special touch of grace for me. The Easter lilies were many and vibrant in symbolism. My son Ryan was enjoying the Presence of the Lord fully now. The night he died, after he had died, I heard him say to me, "Mom, it's so wonderful here – I can hardly wait for you all to come." I kissed the left side of his head for the last time as he lay in the casket and said, "Go and be with our Jesus and pray for us all until we meet again, Son." Our daughters, Mana Rae and Jill, supported me in this action, one on each side. They were there when I needed them. The church was almost full of friends and relatives and people who knew Ryan. I could feel their prayers. Not only was Jesus interceding for us at the right hand of the Father; so were all of them. I felt so lifted up and taken through the pain. As we entered the church and blessed ourselves with holy water, I realized we were asking for the <u>blessing</u> of the Father, Son and Holy Spirit. All He could give us, His all. The song, *You Are Mine*, spoke powerfully to me. He did come to me in the silence. He had embraced all my pain. Jesus called Ryan home and Ryan followed the Lord.

As we all asked Jesus to show us our sins, and confessed them at the Confiteor, I knew he had forgiven me personally for not trusting Him with Ryan's health, 100%. I was so angry when He didn't heal him the way I had hoped He would. Didn't I have enough faith, Jesus? I knew we couldn't lose with Jesus. Either Ryan would be healed on Earth or in Heaven forever. He was healed now forever. I was at Peace. Without His love, there is no pardon for me or my Ryan. He forgave me as in 1 John 1.9, *"He is faithful to forgive all our sins and cleanse us from all unrighteousness."* I was free of all my sins and cleansed by the word and my confession. Then the words of The Creed came: *"I believe in one God, the Father Almighty, Creator of Heaven and Earth..."* I did believe all the church taught and was so grateful for her seeing the whole Bible message and putting it in order for me to rest in and stand on. I believed more fully now *"...in the Holy Catholic Church, the communion of saints, the forgiveness of sins, the resurrection of the body and the life everlasting."*

The Readings were next from *Revelations*. I saw a New Heaven and a New Earth, a New Jerusalem the Lord had prepared Ryan's heart to dwell with Him, and now he is His! He has made all things NEW now. I can rest knowing God is God for him and he is God's son. The Responsorial was *"The Lord is my light and my salvation. Of whom shall I be afraid?"* All I asked was to live in the house of the Lord – all the days of my life. In *Romans*, Shane Mayer read that we are reconciled by Faith in His Blood. Then, the "Alleluias" came for they were not said during Lent and finally we could sing them for it was Easter Time. Praise the Lord for reconciling Ryan by faith in His Blood who is the Lord of Life. We are reconciled also in His Name, the Name above all names. The Church says, "Don't let your hearts be troubled!" Jesus, who is the Way, the Truth and the Life, went to prepare a place for Ryan.

The sermon was given by Ryan and Lori's Parish Priest, Father Anderl, who had witnessed their wedding vows. He had been a Lutheran before he became Catholic, so he helped Lori beautifully into the fullness of the faith. He began with, "Christ is risen, Alleluia. He has conquered death." Jesus our Light conquers the darkness. Jesus won the victory. Death is not an end. Ryan was called to Him. He served the Lord steadily and with great faithfulness. Fr. Anderl and Ryan were good friends and he prayed for Lori with him. One day Ryan called to tell Fr. Anderl he had met this beautiful girl, but she was Lutheran! Fr. Anderl told him he could work with Lori because he had been a Lutheran before he became a Catholic Priest. This was such an answer to prayer for me personally. Just perfect!! Ryan told Father Anderl, "Father, I want you to know we are not living together. I wouldn't dishonor her in that way. Secondly, we go to church every Sunday to get Jesus into our hearts and praise Him; and, thirdly, we won't use contraceptives and will be open to new life as the church tells us to do." Fr. Anderl responded with "Alleluias." In his homily, Fr Anderl emphasized what a joy this couple was to him as a Priest, as they always drew more from him as their shepherd.

The gospel in 1 *Peter* 1:1-9, said, "*Praised be the God and Father of our Lord Jesus Christ. For in his great mercy He gives us a new birth which leads to new hope in all trials.*" For in these trials Ryan was made pure gold. He knew God had to be number one in his life and then, secondly, his family and then his friends. He was only 40 years old; so young to die. But, God called him to Himself. Ryan offered his life for the renewal of married couples. Father Anderl asked the couples to pray that day for any darkness to go away, so all could have holy marriages like Ryan had had that would be pleasing unto the Lord. The church was silent. The Holy

Spirit was present in a powerful way. All felt it. He asked Ryan to pray for all marriages, especially for his parents and siblings. I felt this would be part of his mission.

Also, I hoped, Ryan would pray for the prolife, West First Choice Clinic which had opened that fall in Bismarck, North Dakota. He loved prolife work and did much as a Knight of Columbus. He was especially concerned for girls thinking about having an abortion and so wanted them to get the help they deserved at this clinic and be able to carry their babies to term. Two million couples desire to adopt a baby every year and surgical abortions destroy 1½ million unborn children every year. This indeed is a tragedy and Ryan realized it and prayed and worked to change it. He does it better now in Heaven I am sure. I truly believe that!! After the sermon, I realized I was praying in the Spirit a lot during it. Thank God for that gift. It edified my Spirit and gave me His peace.

The Offertory time came and I had lots to offer to the Lord through my guardian angel who would take all to the throne of God – peace and love for Lori and for their children, first of all; for those who knew Ryan so all could know the Lord as he would want; for his family to be comforted as they all said yes to Jesus and gave their heart 100% to Jesus to live for Him all their days; for the girls who are pregnant so they don't destroy their children, so others can have children to adopt and delight in and bring to the throne of Heaven forever... and, on and on. I wanted my angel to have lots to carry to Jesus.

Then the Miracle of Miracles comes as Jesus wants to be present to us in the bread and the wine. The bread becomes the Body of Jesus so we can be healed. *Isaiah 53.5* says, *"By his stripes we are healed."* He took the pain so I could be free of pain and grief. As I received this gift, I recollected inspirations previously received while praying the Stations of the Cross: *"Three separate times Jesus fell under the heavy weight so I could get up. He carried my sorrows so that I could carry Him in my heart. Bent under the weight of our own cross, I must swallow my pride and allow Him to lift me up to carry my grief. I believed. He did it by the words of the Priest at consecration. The bread is His Body. The wine is His Blood poured out for the remission of my sins. I accept what He did for me on the Cross. Glory to God. I'm free and healed and cleansed. I'm His child in Him."*

As we said the Our Father, I knew He was My Father. I would build His kingdom now in a new way with Ryan interceding for me. I would be more ready to receive my daily bread in faith and forgive more quickly. He would do it in me as I said, "Yes, Change my heart, O God. Make it ever true. Change my heart, O God, may I be like you." I received Him wholly at Holy Communion. I needed <u>all of Him.</u> His Presence was so peaceful. I would see my Ryan again and this sadness will give way to enjoying life everlasting with Jesus and with Ryan and all I loved. The last song, "Lead Me Lord" was perfect for my Spirit as I tried to live the Commandments. The Beatitudes would be the fullness of life for me on this Earth. Blessed are the sorrowing for they would be consoled. Lead me Lord!! I can trust you, Lord.

And, so I trust and hope and believe that God knows best. Someday, I'll see it all the way He does. For today, I ask for the strength to walk closely and hear Jesus' voice, to love deeply my husband, family and friends and to laugh much. Ryan would have me do that. I will be faithful unto Jesus alive in me, who is working in and through me in his Word and in the Sacraments. This is what love looks like.

How Ryan is Now Blessing Me

On October 31, 2011, I drove to see Ryan's widow, Lori, and their children Matthew, 7, Andrew, 4 and Maria, 2½, in Casselton, North Dakota, to enjoy trick-or-treating in their neighborhood. The children's excitement was so heartening for Lori and me as they rushed about and played with neighborhood friends. Small towns can be such a grace as most people know each other and care about people personally. I am so thankful for Lori's many kind and generous neighbors.

As I entered Ryan and Lori's home, it was so hard to go into their garage and see Ryan's Farm House jacket just hanging there on the wall. Suddenly, I so missed him not being there in his body and enjoying his hugs of welcome. I quickly gave it to the Lord, but wanted to somehow feel the pain too! I thought of his children and how they must miss Daddy. I cried to feel the pain Lori must feel not having her loving husband there to love and help discipline the children.

It was a good visit even though it was a brief visit. My sorrow continuously draws me deeper into accepting the will of the Father in this most dear matter and in all parts of my life. I either trust God or I don't, and He has been so good to me and my family in untold multitudes of ways, that I do trust him in this matter, too. This walk with God, trusting Him more and more and more, is a bit like working flour into bread dough. You think what you have worked in must be all it can hold, and then you can work in even more flour. Our Lord wants us to be totally dependent on Him and on his mercy and grace for us and to totally trust him no matter what. It takes a lifetime. Ryan's was short. Mine is much longer and I continue walking on, hand in hand with Jesus, in this world, growing in trust and faith and love. Thanks be to God.

I miss my son. He can never be replaced, but I do know he is with Our Lord and is extremely happy in His Presence. A few weeks after my visit with Lori, I had a dream where I was with my living children, Mana Rae, Jill, Christian and Darwyn. They were all playing together in the snow. As I came closer to see them, Ryan came up to me in his brown, hooded coat and gave me a big, huge hug! Somehow, I know that he knew I needed it! Yes, indeed, he does bless me from Eternity and in mighty ways and I do see his love and blessings go forth to all he loves. Glory to God – Amen and Amen. God knows best. I can trust Him and I do.

I find great peace and understanding in these scriptures, *Colossians* 1:24-29: "Now, I rejoice in my sufferings for your sake, and in my flesh I am filling up what is lacking in the afflictions of Christ on behalf of His Body which is the Church of which I am a minister in accordance with God's stewardship given to me to bring to completion for you the Word of God and the mystery hidden from ages and from generations past. But now it has been manifested in His Holy Ones, to whom God chooses to make known the riches of the Glory of this mystery among the Gentiles: it is Christ in you, the hope of glory! It is He whom we proclaim, admonishing everyone and teaching everyone with all wisdom, that we may present everyone perfect in Christ. For this I labor and struggle, in accord with the exercise of His power working in me."

Every day since Ryan's death I am very aware of how he prays for our marriage. We asked him to intercede. After he did (*Hebrews* 12: 1 and 2), both of us were very tired!! We didn't realize how much energy was going out of us as we grieved for our son. We work long, hard hours on the farm and we are 69 years old and 76 years old already. Both of us had to catch ourselves often and say we were sorry for being irritable toward each other. We would forgive and ask for the grace to grieve healthily and go the extra mile for each other. Sometimes, we would just hold each other and cry our hearts out!! We learned to pray for each other often and Jesus did answer. He is healing us by the power of His Spirit and is giving us what we need as Ryan's Mom and Dad.

Closing Note

I wrote this as a Mother's song, but I could not be a Mother without Ryan's wonderful Father and my most dear Husband, Francis H. Mayer. Our Sacrament of Holy Matrimony is the most precious gift I have ever received from Jesus Christ. Walking all these 46 years, as of August, 2011, hand in hand, on the good farm land the Lord has bless us with, has been the best part of my life. Thank you, Francis, for being the man of God you are and the loving, kind, gentle, faithful and brilliant husband you have been to me.

Delila Mayer,
9446 57th St., SW

Three Years Later... *August 23, 2013*

More of God's grace and mercy in how Ryan's life in Heaven is blessing us.

It is now three years later, and we continue to see God's Hand in why Ryan had to go to Heaven. At the end of Ryan's life – the day before he died – Fr. Anderl gave Ryan the Apostalic Pardon. He had already received the Last Rites of the Church and was in the state of grace. Fr. Anderl prayed, "*Through the holy mysteries of our redemption, may almighty God release you from all punishments in this life and in the life to come. May he open to you the gates of paradise and welcome you to everlasting joy. AMEN."*

I had never heard of this blessing before and was so touched by the church's extension of authority given to those who ask for this grace. I then knew why I saw what I did at the end of Ryan's life. It was a confirmation of where he went with his blessed Mother.

One of the most gracious moments I experienced regarding Ryan going to Jesus was on Mother's Day, just six weeks after he died. I was missing him a lot after I had given Holy Communion to the nursing home people in Mott. It is always a privilege and honor to do so, as I see them so ill but full of faith and gratitude for Jesus who is alive in the tiny host. He wants to heal them and give them His peace and comfort and strength and love in this holy sacrament.[1] He makes Himself present in the Eucharist again.

They understand His real presence, for they know He loves them and cleanses them from all unrighteousness when they are truly sorry. They are healed by His stripes as is in *Isaiah* 53:5 and in *Psalm* 103:3. I always feel I have been blessed

---

[1] *A sacrament is an outward sign instituted by CHRIST to give grace.*

abundantly after I feel this gratitude from each of them. This is not just a piece of bread to them, this is their Jesus!

As I got into the car to go to Mass, I heard him say, "*Happy Mother's Day, Mom.*" I was shocked to hear his voice because I didn't know it was possible! But, then I remembered that Lori Mayer, Ryan's wife, said she received a letter from Bishop Samuel Aquila, who was then her Bishop in Fargo. He said, in essence, that you can't SEE your loved one, but you can HEAR him.

In his letter to Lori, the bishop said, "To the living, I am gone; to the sorrowful, I will never return; to the angry, I was cheated. But to the happy, I am at peace; and to the faithful, I have never left. I cannot be seen, but I can be heard. So as you stand upon a shore, gazing at a beautiful sea, remember me. Remember me in your heart, in your thoughts and the memories of the times we lived, the memories of the times we shared. For if you always think of me, I will have never gone!"

As I heard Ryan's voice, I instantly replied, "*I am so grateful to hear from you, Son, and I am so sorry I couldn't be a perfect mother to you.*"

I heard him say, "*I'm sorry I couldn't be a perfect son for you, but I am NOW!*"

I knew then again why Ryan had to go when he did so. He could pray for all of us perfectly for all our needs. A soft peace enveloped me as I marveled at God's timing. He does make all things beautiful in His time. This is truly what love looks like!

When I spent 11 days with Ryan in Houston, Texas, the Christmas before he died, we spoke of offering up all this pain and the cross for the poor souls in purgatory and for his family to see things the way Jesus did. In *2 Timothy* 1:16-18, *I Corinthians* 3:5 and *Matthew* 5:26 we read about the poor souls in purgatory and how they pray for us as the body of Christ. I had heard that they never forget the ones who pray for them, as they can't pray for themselves.

Ryan's happy death, I believe, was peaceful because of their prayers for him, and I know they came for him also as they got to Heaven at the hour of his death.

Last September 20, 2012, our Diocese of Bismarck, North Dakota, held an Inner Healing Conference at Ascension Catholic Church in Bismarck, North Dakota, with Fr. Larry Carew from Connecticut. Ryan's wife, Lori, came to attend it with us as it was the 10th anniversary of their marriage. Ryan was with us in Spirit and celebrated well with us at the Holy Mass (There is just a veil between us, a very thin veil!) I had seen a friend of mine there whom I did Spiritual Direction with a few years earlier. Two weeks before the conference, she told me she was pregnant and thought she would lose her baby. I introduced her to Lori at the conference, and then she told us she had lost the baby a week previously. We all cried together, and I felt her pain! Praise the Lord she has live children, but the pain is still hard! As I hugged her, I felt the Holy Spirit come through my heart and go down my arms and hands to her, to comfort her. He does that in us. <u>We can heal each other with His LOVE</u>! The next morning, Lori told me, "When I awoke the first thing, I saw Ryan holding a baby! I said let's go tell my friend right now! We all just marveled at God's goodness to this mom, as she realized Ryan was taking care of her baby. She said she knew it was a girl and she named her Mary, the Blessed Mother's name. But, that wasn't the end of the story. That very night, I couldn't sleep. I saw Ryan holding baby after baby and delighting in each one royally. All their gifts he treasured so sweetly.

All of a sudden, I realized these were the aborted babies he had prayed for all his life since he was a young boy. Our Blessed Mother has gone to the trash cans and dumpsters and gathered all of them, taking them to Jesus. And He, by the power of the Spirit, put them together again. Now they have glorified bodies and all in Heaven get to enjoy their gifts, because Love has to be shared in Heaven! These babies are martyr's and are praying for their parents and those who destroyed them to accept the love of Jesus that he gave them on the cross. This Love is free. All of us can't earn it. If they accept this unconditional love and give their hearts to Jesus 100% and are sorry for their sins, they will see their baby in Heaven someday. This is powerful Love, straight from the heart of the Father who made us all like Himself. All they have to do is live for the Lord each day and confess their sins daily, and walk with Him sinless, in purity of heart. What good GOOD news!

We can't save ourselves, but Jesus can, no matter how sinful we all are. There is no sin too big for Jesus not to forgive or heal. And, <u>He delights in being our Savior</u>. This is what He died for... all of our sins. Glory to God!

The girls that have had abortions have been so lied to! They are told this is just a glob of tissue, and in a few minutes it will all be over, and you can go on with your life. I worked for Birthright for 15 years, and would be just sick when a girl decided to destroy her baby! The men in their lives many times would not support them as well as their families. They felt there was no way out but to have the abortion. This industry is big business and Planned Parenthood supports it with our tax dollars. *"The Planned Parenthood Federation of America is the largest abortion provider in the country, and roughly 40% of its one-million dollar budget comes from federal, state and local health service grants and reimbursements."* [2]

There is an organization called Rachel's Vineyard that helps girls who have had an abortion. Also the Saint Gianna's Maternity Home and First Choice Clinic will help girls who need help. Compassionate people donate to these organizations to show the love of Jesus to them. I am including their information at the end of this book.

---

[2] *Carol Tobias, President of National Right to Life, NRL News, Spring 2012*

There are 2-million couples who want to adopt in the U.S. After the conference I attended last fall, someone called to ask me a question. She said, "*Why do I see your face every morning when I get up?*" I said, "*I don't know, but please pray for me when that happens.*" She had an abortion when she was young, and has understood God's love powerfully. I told her the story about Ryan holding babies, and after a long period of time, all she could say was, "*Isn't God good?*" She knew Ryan would take care of her baby till she got there. What Grace!

In short, I can totally let go of Ryan now and trust Our good God with his life. There is nothing so bad that good can't come out of this. *Romans 8:28 says, "All things work together for the good of those who love the Lord and are called according to His purposes."* Is this agape love? YES! YES! YES!

One of Lori's relatives send the following to me. It is precious to my heart as is helps me trust Jesus and His plan for us all:

> *"We seem to give our loved ones back to You, O God, who first gave them to us. But just as You did not lose them in giving, neither do we lose them in returning, for You do not give as the world gives. What you give, You do not take away. You have taught us that what is Yours is ours also if we are Yours. Life is eternal and Your love is undying. Death is only a horizon and a horizon is nothing but the limit of our sight.*
>
> *Lift us up strong Son of God that we may see farther. Cleanse our eyes that we may see more clearly. Draw us closer to Yourself, O Lord, that we may find ourselves closer to You and to our loved ones who are with You. And while You prepared a place for them, prepare us also for that happy place where You are and where we hope to be forever."*
>
> AMEN
>
> *Anonymous text from a Benedictine prayer book*

Please join us in prayer now with Ryan in Heaven for the world to have Godly sorrow for our sins that leads us to true repentence, and accept what Jesus did on the cross for everyone as pure love and grace, so we can all be together at the end, glorifying the Lord of Lords and King of Kings. All He wants is our hearts, 100%, so He can work in and through us. If we seek Him in every situation, and want to please Him above all else, we will find Him and the answer. Even if it is very very hard, He will be there with His peace that passes all understanding. Always remember, forgiving an enemy sets the prisoner free... and that prisoner is me. May we all pray for each other to glorify the Lord and live in His ways.

See you in Heaven.
Delila Mayer

Mott, ND 58646
701-824-2381

APPENDIX

Praying in the Spirit, in Tongues

"Praying in the spirit, in tongues" is one of many gifts the Holy Spirit gives. Many Christians, many Charismatic Christians and many Catholic Charismatic Christians have and do experience this gift. For many it is a natural part of their very meaningful, intimate friendship and prayer life with Jesus Christ. See *Mark* 16:17; I *Corinthians* 12; I *Corinthians* 14:1-5; *Acts* 2; *Acts* 19:6; *Romans* 8:26-27; *Jude* 20. Also, if interested, seek out Charismatic Christians and hear their testimonies.

Efficacious Novena to the Sacred Heart of Jesus
(Padre Pio recited this Novena every day for all those who asked for his prayers.)

O my Jesus, you have said: "Truly I say to you, ask and it will be given you, seek and you will find, knock and it will be opened to you." Behold I knock, I seek and ask for the grace of...

Our Father...Hail Mary...Glory be to the Father...Sacred Heart of Jesus, I place all my trust in You.

O my Jesus, You have said: "Truly I say to you, if you ask anything of the Father in my name, He will give it to you." Behold, in Your name, I ask the Father for the grace of...

Our Father...Hail Mary...Glory be to the Father...Sacred Heart of Jesus, I place all my trust in You.

O my Jesus, you have said: "Truly I say to you, heaven and Earth will pass away, but my words will not pass away." Encouraged by Your infallible words, I now ask for the grace of...
Our Father...Hail Mary...Glory be to the Father...Sacred Heart of Jesus, I place all my trust in you.

O Sacred Heart of Jesus, for whom it is impossible not to have compassion on the afflicted, have pity on us sinners, and grant us the grace which we ask of You, through the Sorrowful and Immaculate Heart of Mary, Your tender Mother and ours.

Pray the "Hail, Holy Queen."

Conclude with:
St. Joseph, foster father of Jesus, pray for us.
(You are invited to recite this prayer daily, so as to be spiritually united with the prayer of Saint Pio.)

St. Therese of the Child Jesus: My Novena Rose Prayer

O Little Therese of the Child Jesus, please pick for me a rose from the heavenly gardens and send it to me as a message of love. O Little Flower of Jesus, ask God today to grant the favors I now place with confidence in your hands.... (Mention specific requests)
St. Therese, help me to always believe as you did, in God's great love for me, so that I might imitate your "Little Way" each day.
Amen.

The Chaplet of the Divine Mercy
(to be recited on ordinary rosary beads)

After crossing yourself, begin with:
Our Father..., Hail Mary ..., The Apostle's Creed.

Then, on the OUR FATHER BEADS (for all 5 decades) you will say the following words:
Eternal Father, I offer You the Body and Blood, Soul and Divinity of Your dearly beloved Son, Our Lord Jesus Christ, in atonement for our sins and those of the whole world.
On the HAIL MARY BEADS (for all 5 decades) you will say the following words:
For the sake of His sorrowful Passion, have mercy on us and on the whole world.

In conclusion, THREE TIMES you will recite these words:
Holy God, Holy Mighty One, Holy Immortal One, have mercy on us and on the whole world.

Litany of the Saints

(Cantor)   (All)

Lord, have mercy.   **Lord, have mercy.**
Christ, have mercy.   **Christ, have mercy.**
Lord, have mercy.   **Lord, have mercy.**

Holy Mary, Mother of God,	***Pray for us.***
Holy Angels of God,	Saint Gregory,
Saint John the Baptist,	Saint Augustine,
Saint Joseph,	Saint Athanasius,
Saint Peter and Saint Paul,	Saint Basil,
Saint Andre,	Saint Martin,
Saint John	Saint Benedict,
Saint Mary Magdalene,	Saint Francis & Saint Dominic,
Saint Stephen,	Saint Francis Xavier,
Saint Ignatius of Antioch,	Saint John Vianney
Saint Lawrence,	Saint Catherine of Siena,
Saint Perpetua & Saint Felicity,	Saint Teresa of Jesus,
Saint Agnes,	All holy men and women, Saints of God,

Lord, be merciful,	***Lord, deliver us, we pray.***
From all evil,	***Lord, deliver us, we pray.***
From every sin,	***Lord, deliver us, we pray.***
From everlasting death,	***Lord, deliver us, we pray.***
By your Incarnation,	***Lord, deliver us, we pray.***
By your Death & Resurrection,	***Lord, deliver us, we pray.***
By the outpouring of the Holy Spirit,	***Lord, deliver us, we pray.***

Be merciful to us sinners,	***Lord, we ask you, hear our prayer.***
Jesus, Son of the Living God,	***Lord, we ask you, hear our prayer.***

Christ, hear us. Christ, graciously hear us.
Amen

The Miracle Prayer

Lord Jesus, I come before You, just as I am. I am sorry for my sins. I repent of my sins, please forgive me. In Your name I forgive all others for what they have done against me. I renounce Satan, the evil spirits and all their works. I give you my entire self, Lord Jesus, now and forever. I invite You into my life, Jesus, I accept You as my Lord, God and Savior. Heal me, change me, strengthen me in body, soul and spirit.

Come Lord Jesus, cover me with Your precious blood, and fill me with Your Holy Spirit. I love You, Lord Jesus. I praise You, Jesus. I thank You, Jesus. I shall follow You every day of my life.
Amen

Mary my mother, Queen of peace, all the Angels and Saints, please help me.
Amen

Prayer of Consecration to the Holy Spirit

O Holy Spirit, divine Spirit of light and love,
I consecrate to You my intellect, my heart,
My will and my whole being for time and for eternity.
May my intellect be ever docile to Your heavenly inspirations and to the teaching of the Holy Catholic Church of which You are the infallible Guide.
May my heart be ever inflamed with the love of God and my neighbor; may my will be ever in conformity with the divine will, and may my whole life be a faithful imitation of the life and virtues of our Lord and Savior Jesus Christ, to whom, with the Father and You, Holy Spirit, be honor and glory forever.
Amen

(Say this prayer faithfully, no matter how you feel. When you come to the point where you sincerely mean each word, with all your heart, something good spiritually will happen to you. You will experience Jesus, and He will change your whole life in a very special way. You will see. *Fr. Peter Mary Rookey, OSM*)

Prayer of St. Gertrude, the Great

Eternal Father, I offer Thee the Most Precious Blood of Thy Divine Son, Jesus, in union with the Masses said throughout the world today, for all the holy Souls in Purgatory, for sinners everywhere, for sinners in the Universal Church, those in my own home and within my family. Amen
JESUS, JESUS, JESUS

(Our Lord told St. Gertrude, the Great, that this prayer would release 1,000 Souls from Purgatory each time it is said. The prayer was extended to include living sinners which would alleviate the indebtedness accrued to them during their lives.)

Consecration to the Eternal Father

For the greater glory of God and for the salvation of all, I Consecrate myself to You, O Eternal Father, as one of your faithful remnant. Behold, I come to do Your Will. With the help of Your Grace,
I will keep Your Commandments. I will love and reverence You with all
My heart, soul, mind and strength. I will love my neighbor as You Love me.
I make this consecration through the Immaculate Heart of Mary and the Sacred Heart of Your beloved Son, Jesus.
O Eternal Father, send forth Your Holy Spirit to restore our broken image and likeness of You.
Send forth also the celestial choirs of Your angels to aid us in our struggle against all the forces of evil in this present darkness.
Amen

Come, Holy Spirit

Replace the tension within us with a holy relaxation.
Replace the turbulence within us with a sacred calm.
Replace the anxiety within us with a quiet confidence.
Replace the fear within us with a strong faith.
Replace the bitterness within us with the sweetness of Your grace.
Replace the darkness within us with a gentle light.
Replace the coldness within us with a loving warmth.
Replace the night within us with Your day.
Replace the winter within us with Your Spring.
Straighten our crookedness;
Fill our emptiness,
Dull the edge of our pride,
Sharpen the edge of our humility,
Light the fires of our love.
Let us see ourselves as You see us,
that we may see You as You have promised.
Amen

A Secret of Sanctity

(I am going to reveal to you a secret of sanctity and happiness. If every day during five minutes, you will keep your imagination quiet, shut your eyes to all the things of sense, and close your ears to all the sounds of Earth, so as to be able to withdraw into the sanctuary of your baptized soul, which is the temple of the Holy Spirit, speaking there to that Holy Spirit saying):

O Holy Spirit, soul of my soul, I adore You. Enlighten, guide, strengthen and console me. Tell me what I ought to do and command me to do it. I promise to be submissive in everything that You permit to happen to me, only show me what is your will.

(If you do this, your life will pass happily and serenely. Consolation will abound even in the midst of troubles. Grace will be given in proportion to the trial as well as strength to bear it, bringing you to the gates of Paradise full of merit.)

This submission to the Holy Spirit is the Secret of Sanctity.
— Cardinal Mercier

Prayer to St. Michael

St. Michael the Archangel, defend us in battle.
Be our protection against the wickedness and snares of the Devil.
May God rebuke him, we humbly pray.
And, do thou, O Prince of the heavenly host,
by the power of God,
cast into hell Satan and all the evil spirits,
who prowl about the world seeking the ruin of souls.
Amen

Angel of God

Angel of God, my guardian dear,
Whose God's love commits thee here,
Ever this day, be at my side,
To light, to guard, to rule and guide.
Amen

Healing Prayer at Bedtime

Jesus, through the power of the Holy Spirit, go back into my memory as I sleep. Every hurt that has ever been done to me – heal that hurt.
Every hurt that I have ever caused to another person – heal that hurt.
All the relationships that have been damaged in my whole life that I'm not aware of – heal those relationships.
But, Lord, if there is anything that I need to do – if I need to go to a person because he is still suffering from my hand, bring to my awareness that person.
I choose to forgive, and I ask to be forgiven. Remove whatever bitterness may be in my heart, Lord, and fill the empty spaces with your love. Thank you, Jesus.
Amen

O, Jesus

O, Jesus, in union with your most precious blood poured out on the cross and offered in every mass, I offer you today my prayers, works, joys, sorrows and sufferings for the praise of your holy name and all the desires of your sacred heart; in reparation for sin, for the conversion of sinners, the union of all Christians and our final union with you in heaven.

Surrender Prayer

I kneel again this day to say, I am a servant of the Most High God.
His Son, Jesus Christ, is my Lord,
and I bow to declare His authority over my life.
I lift my hands to You, O Father, and pray,
"Come Holy Spirit and fill me this day to glorify Jesus."
Amen

Prayer of Thanksgiving for the Holy Spirit

Jesus, I know now that I am yours and you are mine forever.
I thank you for sending your Spirit to me
that I might have the power to live this new life with you.
Stir up your Spirit in me.
Release your Spirit in me.
Baptize me with the fullness of your Spirit
that I may experience your presence and power in my life,
that I may find new meaning in your Scriptures,
that I may find new meaning in the sacraments,
that I may find delight and comfort in prayer,
that I may be able to love as you love and forgive as you forgive,
that I may discover and use the gifts you give me for the life of the Church,
that I may experience the peace and the joy that you have promised us.
Fill me with your Spirit, Jesus.
I wish to receive all that you have to give me.
Amen.

The Spirit in Me

Jesus, I know now that I am yours and you are mine forever.

I thank you for sending your Spirit to me

> *that I might have the power to live this new life with you.*

Stir up your spirit in me.

Release your Spirit in me.

Baptize me with the fullness of your Spirit

> *that I may experience your presence and power in my life,*
>
> *that I may find new meaning in your Scriptures,*
>
> *that I may find new meaning in the sacraments*
>
> *that I may find delight and comfort in prayer,*
>
> *that I may be able to love as you love and to forgive as you forgive,*
>
> *that I may discover and use the gifts you give me for the life of the church,*
>
> *that I may experience the peace and the joy that you have promised us.*

Fill me with your Spirit, Jesus.

I wish to receive all that you have to give me.

Amen

Prayer to the Wounds of Christ

(N.B. It is of the utmost importance to be aware that you are speaking to JESUS himself when you say these prayers and in that awareness, one should pray with great reverence and devotion in all humility.)

My Jesus pardon and mercy through the merits of Your most sacred wounds. *(To be repeated 10 times after each sacred wound.)*

I kiss the wounds of your sacred hands with sorrow deep and true. May every touch of my hands be an act of love for you. Jesus, I give you my hands to serve you.

I kiss the wounds of Your sacred head with sorrow deep and true. May every thought in my mind be an act of love for You. I invite You now, Lord Jesus, to come into my mind. Let Your healing light shine into every corner of my mind to dispel the darkness in my mind. Let Your healing light shine into my past. Fill my mind with Your healing light and uplift me now in a very special way. Fill every thought I've ever had in my mind with Your healing light. Heal my memories, thought patterns, mindsets and conditioning. Come into my anger, anxiety, fear, worries, hurts, sadness, etc. Come into all my relationships, especially where there is healing needed, and give those people great blessings and, most of all, give them peace of mind.

I kiss the wounds of Your sacred shoulder with sorrow deep and true, I offer up to You all the crosses I have had in my life especially the cross that I struggle with at the present moment *(mention)*, for the conversion of the sinners, the souls in purgatory and also the most forgotten souls.

I kiss the wounds of Your sacred side with sorrow deep and true. May every beat of my heart be an act of love for You and by the merits of that wound to Your most sacred side, please fill my heart with a much greater love for You, a much greater trust in You that You are healing me right now and filling me with love and compassion for all.

I kiss the wounds of Your sacred heart with sorrow deep and true, I ask You now, Lord Jesus, to take me and everyone in my life into Your sacred heart, cover us with Your precious blood and protect us. Our Lady cover us with your blue mantle and protect us.

I kiss the wounds of Your sacred feet with sorrow deep and true. May every step I take be an act of love for You. I ask You now, Lord Jesus, to guide my steps in the direction that best serves my soul and the will of God.

Eternal Father, I offer You the most sacred wounds of **Our Lord Jesus Christ** to heal the wounds of our souls.

Please light a candle to comfort me in the Garden of Gethsemane and to honour my Sacred Wounds.

Wasted Pain
By Rev. Fulton J. Sheen

There is nothing more tragic in all the world than wasted pain. Think of how much suffering there is in hospitals, among the poor and bereaved. Think also of how much of that suffering goes to waste.

How many of those lonesome, suffering, abandoned, crucified souls are saying with our Lord at themoment of Consecration: "This is my body, take it?" And yet that is what we should be saying at that second. "Here is my body, take it. Here is my soul, my will, my energy, my strength, my poverty, my wealth – ALL that I have. It is Yours. Take it! Consecrate it! Offer it to the Heavenly Father with Yourself, in order that He, looking down on this great Sacrifice, may see only You, His beloved Son, in whom He is well-pleased. Transmute the poor bread of my life into Your Life; thrill the wine of my wasted life into Your divine Spirit; unite my broken heart with Your Heart; change my cross into a crucifix. Let not my abandonment and my sorrow go to waste. Gather up the fragments, and as the drop of water is absorbed by the wine at the Offeratory of the Mass, let my life be absorbed in You. Let my little cross be entwined with Your great cross so that I may purchase the joys of everlasting happiness in union with You.

"Consecrate these trials of my life which would go unrewarded unless united with You; transubstantiate me so that, like bread which is now Your Body, and wine which is now Your Blood, I, too, may be wholly Yours. I care not if the species remain, or that, like the bread and wine, I may seem to all earthly eyes the same as before. My station in life, my routine duties, my work, my family – all these are but species of my life which may remain unchanged; but the substance of my life, my soul, my will, my heart, transsubstantiate them, transform them wholly into Your service so that through me all may know how sweet is the love of Christ!"

Rachel's Vineyard - *Healing the pain of abortion, one weekend at a time.*
   808 N. Henderson Road
   King of Prussia, PA 19406
   610-354-0555 / fax 610-354-0311
   Hotline: 1-877-HOPE-4-ME (1-877-467-3463)
   http://www.rachelsvineyard.org

Saint Gianna's Maternity Home - *Serving the body of Christ as a pro-life residential shelter for pregnant women and their children.*
   15605 County Road 15
   Minto, ND 58261
   701-248-3077 / 1-877-701.3077
   http://www.saintgiannahome.com
   email: saintgiannahome@hotmail.com

FirstChoice Clinics in Fargo, Bismarck and Devils Lake, North Dakota
   1-888-237-6530
   http://www.firstchoiceclinic.com

Special thanks to my kinswoman, Hildy Boespflug, wife of Dr. Randy Boespflug, originally from the Richardton, North Dakota, area who now lives in Florence, Oregon. She collected, typed, edited, advised and prayed with me.

Also, special thanks to Pat Edwards of *Groundwaters* Publishing, LLC. She formulated and published this book and can be reached at:
   P.O. Box 50, Lorane, OR 97451; 541-344-0986
   http://www.groundwaterspublishing.com

Made in the USA
San Bernardino, CA
29 September 2013